The Write Edit

by
Dawn Blair

Morning Sky Studios

The Write Edit

Text and cover art by
Dawn Blair

Morning Sky Studios
P.O. Box 5422
Twin Falls, ID 83301

Visit us online at
www.morningskystudios.com

ISBN: 978-0-9830905-6-4

Contents

Introduction

It's all about the story. Your story.

The act of writing is a personal experience. Stories come from our heads and our hearts. Many times the tales and characters are closer to us than anyone else we know.

Since you're reading this book, I know you're serious about writing fiction. What I don't know is where you're at on your writer's journey. Whether you are a novice or a multi-published, best-selling author, I hope you find benefit from my humble undertaking. Even if you've heard everything stated in this book, reiteration is never a bad thing. In the end, I want you to understand how to tell a better story.

Over the years, I've seen a movement, if it can be called that, toward telling a story instead of showing a story. Every how-to book and writing magazine is crying out, "Show your story. Here's how you do it." Still, I put down a majority of books after reading page one. Yes, on that very first page I know if a writer has learned their craft and understands the depth enough to put it into practice. My question has become: If I know this, then why don't the editors publishing their books realize this?

My answer is simple. Editors are too busy with meetings convincing everyone else at the publishing house to carry their book instead of another editor's book that they no longer have time to edit. The editor has to be <u>told</u> a good story in order to <u>tell</u> others. The easier the story is to tell, the easier it is to sell.

I'm taking an opinionated stand against

this crime violating the readers of the world. It's my wish that eventually this book makes its way to every editor's desk for a quick reference. Until then, I have to make sure the author's submitting their babies to the publishing houses possess the best manuscript they can craft.

Unlike other editing books, this one will not teach you about grammar, punctuation or anything of the sort. Instead, it focuses solely your story and how to make it better by fixing the words.

I 'm not an editor, though I have judged several writing contests on local, state-wide, and national levels. I am a writer. I've been telling stories since I was four years old. I grew up composing tales in every free moment I found. I've had several great critique partners over the years and I hope they've learned as much from me as I have from them. Mostly, I've spent a lot of time writing and thinking about the art of writing. These are my discoveries. If you've made different ones, I'd certainly love to hear them.

Here are a few writing books I'd like to recommend at this point. If you haven't read them, don't feel like you need to rush out and do so before you finish this.

➢ *The Key* by James Frey
➢ *The Writer's Journey* by Christopher Vogler
➢ *Sometimes the Magic Works: Lessons from a Writing Life* by Terry Brooks
➢ *The 10% Solution* by Ken Rand
➢ *Techniques of the Selling Writer* by Dwight Swain

What is a story and how do I get one?

The advice for writing your first draft is simple: Just write it.

Get your ideas down on paper. Don't worry about character consistency or if you suddenly have a gaping hole in your plot that you could drive a Hummer through. Don't worry if your character decides to start going by another name (though you might want to either make a note of the change so you don't confuse yourself later or use your Find/Replace function on your word processor to change the name). Don't worry if you suddenly change genres.

Think of this step as the archaeological step in writing. You're going to dig a lot of holes while you're looking for the pyramid. The problem is that it's easy to get stuck in one of these holes, hit ground bottom, and keep digging.

Don't get me wrong here. Occasionally exploratory digging is necessary. I'll use my own story, Sacred Knight, as an example. Over many years, I've written four complete drafts, each one slightly different, and eight more partial manuscripts. I have at least 20 different beginnings for this story. Sometimes I've been stuck in a single hole refusing to get out because I knew if I dug three more feet I'd find the pyramid of enlightenment. Was all this digging worth it?

Yes.

Sacred Knight is a fantasy where I've made the entire world up, which meant building everything: culture, history, religion, politics, etc.

On top of that, I had three different time lines, but I didn't realize that until I'd written massive amounts of material. It changed genres a couple times and is finally taking shape as a graphic novel. Even now that I know the story, I still get little insights into the world.

The point is: write until you feel like you have a handle on the story. One draft may do it. Three drafts and several short stories might be needed for another. Just keep at it until you have the story.

How do you know when you have the story?

The dictionary defines story as an account of incidents or events. Wrong! An account of incidents or events is boring. It might as well be a soap opera where it doesn't have to make sense and incidents/events just keep happening. A good story demonstrates how a character faces danger.

I'll say that again: a story is how a

character faces danger.

When I tell this to other writers I get an appalled look in response. They instantly think "danger" has to mean life or death, or high-action adventure with car chases and guns blazing. They don't write THAT kind of fiction.

Let's get this straight. Danger is <u>any</u> obstacle that stands in the way of your character getting his/her goal.

If your female character has a cheating husband and she wants to keep her family together, she faces the "danger" of having her family torn apart. If your hero needs to bring the Elixir of Life back to his village but the evil witch doesn't want him to get there in time, he faces a "danger". The teenager from 1868 faces "danger" when she runs away to find her mountaineer father.

Let's look a little more in-depth at these three examples.

The woman with the cheating husband

can have several obstacles that heighten her danger. She may have two mortgages on the farm and ownership of this land is symbolic of her family. No land, no family. Money might disappear from the bank account as the husband drains it to spend on his girlfriends and makes it harder for the woman to make the monthly payments. Husband can come home with a sexually transmitted disease, now there are medical bills in addition to trying to keep the horrible truth from the children.

The hero with the elixir has to return by the second moon after he leaves. His horse might throw a shoe. A hedgerow of thorns may spring up around the village. He could be poisoned by berries he was told were safe to eat by a "kindly" old woman. He may discover a crack in the container with the elixir and wonder if it's still good. Magically created monsters stalk his every move.

The runaway teenager might face false

leads, Indians, and unfriendly wagon drivers. She may have stolen the bit of little money she carries. She could meet a man who promises her the world if she'll work on sewing his clothes and finds herself unable to get away from him.

Look at stories or movies you've been reading or watching lately. Look for the danger faced by those characters. It's a simple contraption once you understand it.

Your main character has to want something. Everyone wants something. When you know what the character wants, you'll know if it's a long term or a short term goal. Most stories are built on one of these types of goals or the other. On rare occasions, it'll be both. Generally it's a short term goal.

In Sacred Knight, my character's long term goal is to have a family but it's a bare mention in the story. His short term goal consists of finding three books and that's where he faces his danger.

Once you know the goal, set obstacles in the path to keep your character from getting there and each roadblock adds to the dangers. That's your story.

At this point writers start complaining, "But my story is character-driven."

Have you heard about "a character-driven story versus a plot-driven story" before? Hate to tell you this, especially if you're a writer who has said this to someone before, but there is no such thing.

A plot-driven story is one where the characters are cardboard two-dimensional and full of car chases, explosions, or other high action devices meant to lure the reader into feeling an adrenalin rush. A character-driven story is one where the two-dimensional characters are tossed around on a sea created by a God-Author where everyone is weeping and sad and distraught to forget that there is no plot. In both, they are just events happening to the characters so the characters can react with a fight (plot-driven) or flight (character-driven).

Now that you know the two ends of the spectrum, aim for the truth which is that all good stories are *story-driven*. The balance between these two extreme ends is a plot and believable reactions from the characters. Neither plot nor reactions are forced upon the characters, but come from within the character. While you yourself are full of contradictions, you would still never swing into a reaction too far outside your own character. If you are steadfast against drinking, you aren't going to go down to the bar and get sloshing drunk just because you had a bad day. Grab a box of chocolate ice cream maybe, even though you've been dieting for two months. So, now you know the difference, aim for a story-driven story. Leave the rest of the excuses behind with less skilled writers.

Once your draft is written and you know where your story is going, you have one more step before down and dirty editing: to know where your passion comes from for the story. Do you want your reader to love the main character as much as you do? Do you want your reader to feel the same thrill for the adventure as you do? Or maybe you want to step out of this world and into the milieu you created and live the rest of your life there. Once you identify the element that pulls you to this story, write the reason down somewhere. You don't necessarily need to put it right in front of you, but somewhere you can refer to it when you feel drained of energy and you want throw the story out. Or burn it. Or throw it from the nearest bridge. It helps if you can recall the passion that drives and keeps you at the story.

Where do I start editing?

At this point, you have a manuscript, you know what the story is, and you know your passion for telling the story. Now the work begins to make the story great.

Start by writing a one to two page single-spaced synopsis. Don't be shy. Reveal all the details, especially if it's a mystery plot. Show how the villain gets caught. Chances are this isn't the synopsis you'll use in the end, so think of this as a practice run. You're merely summing up the story for yourself.

Feel free to look back at your manuscript to remember the order of events. This isn't a pop quiz. Again, this is something only you will see.

The vital thing is that it's no more than two single-spaced pages long.

Once you're done, put it away and go reward yourself. Get away from the synopsis and story overnight at least. I realize you're probably chomping to get going on your edit, but distance is important at this point. You'll need a clear head when you come back. So take a break. If you really want to keep writing, work on another story, something totally unconnected to it.

When you've had a chance to clear the story out of your head and feel like you can come back with a fresh perspective, read through the synopsis and ask yourself one question: Is this a story or is it a series of events?

Don't let your passion for the story confuse you. Too many times when editing a story, we become enthralled with the words. It takes us into the story and we can't see the writing anymore. Stay focused on the words themselves. If someone was telling you this synopsis, would you view it as one character's struggle to reach a goal, or as a series of events more like a soap opera.

If you come away thinking it's a series of events, go back to the last chapter of this book and review how to find the danger your character faces and keep fleshing it out. Your story isn't mature enough yet and you may need to do some more digging. Chances are once you have all the elements, the rest of the story will pop into focus. You can then rewrite your synopsis with this new spirit.

If your synopsis' strength confirms your story, it's time to move forward.

So what's next? Your research. That should be something you've worked on while writing your first draft, but maybe not. I've always found it easiest to research while I write and that way I know what I'm going to need. Sometimes I'll use placeholder cues to know where I need to dig a little deeper with research. Once you have your synopsis done, you should know exactly what you need to do for your research.

Start small. Children's books and documentaries are often great places to get general overviews on all sorts of topics. I find it easier to listen and watch my research than it is to read it sometimes. Don't, however, assume that just because you see something in your favorite TV show or movie that it's accurate information. Way too many shows feature a bad guy who waves a gun around and fires while his whole arm is relaxed. Or the attorney gets up and starts walking around the courtroom. Oh, it's great for action. Not good for keeping a reader willing to suspend disbelief. If you get these things inaccurate they'll start keeping an eye out for other holes. Too many and they'll put your book down and walk away.

Do the research, even if it's hard. There's

lots of information on the Internet. If you write about guns but have never fired one, find a friend who has and have them take you out on a range or where ever they like to go target shooting and actually fire one. You'll be surprised and Internet research will never fill you in on what it's actually like to feel the kick of a gun in your hands. It's something you must experience if you want to write about it. Some topics need that kind of research and others don't. But whatever your story needs, get out there and do it. This is where knowing where your passion for the story comes in handy – to give you courage to ask for help.

The next thing is your time line. Even though your story shouldn't be just a series of events, the sequence of obstacles should be logical. Stimulus has to have a response. Those reactions cause other events to happen (see Dwight Swain's book <u>Techniques of the Selling Writer</u> for an in-depth analysis of this chain).

Make sure you have A, then B, then C. Your synopsis will probably point these errors out to you, but now is the opportunity to double check.

Now we start fleshing out the hero of the tale and developing the other characters by deciding how each interacts with the other. Once you're done this exercise, the characters won't feel like they are standing side by side in a line, but rather like one big net cast around the main character.

Every member of the cast needs to have his or her own motivation. Again, everyone wants something. And, everybody hides a secret they don't want anyone else to know. It's common when a neighborhood finds out that they've had a killer living among them to say, "I didn't know. He was such a nice man. I never imagined." Look hard enough at yourself and you'll find your own deep dark secret. Once you find yours, it'll be easier to uncover your main character's secret. Watch people to see what they disclose to others (while keeping in mind that they will never completely reveal themselves) and you'll find motivations for the other characters in your book.

There's a good chance most of these will never be divulged in your book. The purpose of a deep, dark, secret is to keep it hidden. But it will influence how a character behaves and how much he or she will expose to the outside world. The more you know about the inner workings of a character, even if it's never all shown, the more real the character will seem to the reader.

It takes years to develop the human personality. Why would you spend only a few minutes creating the villain who takes on your main character?

With everything fleshed out, now is the time to rewrite the full plot synopsis. Compile all the notes you've taken through this process so that nothing gets lost, read through your notes, and then start writing the synopsis. This isn't going to follow your original synopsis, but the amount it deviates from your original synopsis depends on how far you varied during your discovery process.

Don't beat yourself up if you feel like you strayed so far that you don't recognize your original plot, or if you feel like you've done a lot of work for nothing. Neither of these is true! Every moment of hard work is shaping you into a better author. That's why we're here, remember?

This is your time to make sure the plot is tight and holds water. Keep an eye out for holes. Make sure your point of view is with the appropriate character. I'll go over point of view in more depth later, but right now just make sure you have a single point of view.

Finally, once you've gotten the second synopsis done, you need to ask yourself a very important question: Does the manuscript need to be rewritten entirely?

If you're answering yes, I hope you're excited about it rather than slumping your shoulders in defeat. This is a good moment to remember the passion for your story. Then, jump into it. This time you have your guideposts. You know the story so you don't have to stray. The synopsis becomes the bones for your story. You'll still find surprising things along the way. Enjoy the journey.

If your draft is pretty much intact and you only need to rewrite sections of it, get this taken care of before continuing on. Don't worry, I'll wait.

Point of View:

Whose story is this?

For the remainder of the book, I'll give illustrative examples and we'll correct them step by step. Near the end of this book, you'll find a practice sample for you to edit. The "answers" will be the final thing. I say "answers" because fortunately for all of us, writing is a subjective art and my answers don't have to be your answers. But it will give you hands-on experience that most editing books don't dare tackle.

Here's the first passage:

Sara was a plain woman of average height. She tucked a hair into her bun as she passed by the reflective store window. I do need a haircut, she thought. Turning the cold knob in her hand, she entered the salon.

"How can I help you?" greeted a lady coming up to the counter while chewing a piece of gum. She rubbed her hands on her apron and looked Sara over, thinking this woman needed a makeover and quick.

A dog, a chocolate lab looked up from his bed over in the corner. No danger here. He went back to chewing on his bone.

Let's dissect this little segment of a story typical of writing I've seen in contests and it's full of problems. Let's start with the point of view.

The first sentence is spoken outside the character like someone observing her. Sara may think she's plain, but how often do we think of ourselves in third person. If this were Sara's point of view, it would've been written, '*I*'*m so plain*, Sara thought as she walked by the store window.' The second sentence is a step closer to Sara, but the reader isn't in Sara's thoughts either. Finally, the third sentence is in Sara's point of view because we're given her thoughts of needing a haircut.

While I have taken this to the extreme here, it's a good example of how to move a camera in on a character in a cinematic fashion. This is an effective technique to use when you're transitioning between scenes or even between characters, provided that you use the camera technique to move away from the first point of view character and then back in to a second point of view character. The major problem here is the jump from third person to first person with the thoughts. The reader has gone from being completely outside the character to – Wham! - inside the character within three sentences. Head jumping is a bumpy ride for the reader.

A quick example:

His cold temperament upset Alice and she turned away. Brad, sensing her anger, took her arm and turned her around. He felt badly for what he'd said but didn't know how to show her. The kiss he swept her up in made the train conductor turn uncomfortably away.

First Alice is *upset*, but Brad senses it. That's one head jump. We continue in Brad's head because he *felt badly*. He tried to make his kiss an apology which embodies all his unspoken emotion and that makes the train conductor *uncomfortable* – how would Alice and Brad know the conductor was uncomfortable especially since they're locked in this kiss so it's got to be the conductor's point of view.

This is why it's important to know which character faces the danger and tell your story from that character's point of view.

Going back to the first example, if Sara is the main character, the better paragraph would have written as:

Sara tucked a hair into her bun, thinking how plain she'd become over the last few years. The reflective store window acted like a mirror to illustrate this point. Maybe she needed a change, a haircut perhaps. Something younger, not so time-worn. Turning the cold knob in her hand, she entered the salon.

I admit that I jazzed this up a bit to keep the important points, but it illustrates how easy it is to add details if you're firmly in a point of view. The reader still knows that Sara thinks she's plain and that she's thinking about getting a haircut, all without outside interference or first person thoughts. Throughout the passage, the reader is firmly in Sara's head.

The second paragraph jumps to the hairdresser's point of view with 'thinking this woman needed a makeover." Did you catch it? Wouldn't it be so much better if Sara just thought the woman was judging Sara? Wouldn't that sting Sara's already sore self-esteem? This could be particularly poignant if part of Sara's danger involved her low self-esteem (the argument could be made that if her danger doesn't involve her self-esteem, why is this even in the book, but that's another issue we'll get to later).

The last paragraph is the dog's point of view. Yes, that's right. Read it again looking very carefully at the words, not the story. We jumped into the dog's head!

Let's fix this:

Sara tucked a hair into her bun, thinking how plain she'd become over the last few years. The reflective store window acted like a mirror to illustrate this point. Maybe she needed a change, a haircut perhaps. Something younger and not so time-worn. Turning the cold knob in her hand, she entered the salon.

"How can I help you?" greeted a lady coming up to the counter. She snapped her gum as she rubbed her hands on her apron and looked Sara over, a sneer nearly formed on her lips.

Sara resisted the urge to run out, away from the hairdresser's judgmental gaze.

A chocolate Labrador looked up from his bed over in the corner, gave a snort, and went back to chewing on his bone. Even he, Sara realized, knew that this plain Jane wasn't bringing in any danger.

That last sentence, without 'Sara realized,' would've slipped back into the dog's point of view. Cover up those words with your finger and read it again to see what I mean. By adding these two little words we keep it in Sara's point of view.

Now that you've got the basics of point of view, let's talk about the God-Author. It used to be fashionable to have the Author on high talking to the reader. "Gentle reader, take my hand and let me lead you on this journey..." God-Author uses phrases like, 'Sara's mother was a round woman, though not particularly jolly as most people expect round people to be.' Here, Sara's mother equals a round woman. Any time that you have 'was' becoming an equal sign, you should question it. It's your first clue that something is horribly wrong. The second clue that you've had God-Author step in is the heavy voice that enters with 'though not particularly jolly as most people expect.' It's telling the story, not showing the story. 'Was' is an indicator of telling a story and we'll discuss it more in-depth later.

In nearly every contest I've judged, at least one entry has a God-Author. It's fine and expected if you're writing non-fiction, especially in self-help or how-to. This book is written with a God-Author perspective for example. It's hard to get away from in non-fiction. However, with fiction, it's extremely hard to pull off. You've got to have an angle. Most of the time it is in humorous fiction. But if your humor isn't there and your God-Author is coming across as arrogant, you're going to turn your reader away. If you want to see how God-Author can be effective, read *The Hitchhiker's Guide to the Galaxy* by Douglas Adams. He has a sporadic narrative voice that intrudes upon the story – this is the God-Author coming in. Watch the cinematic style Adams uses to handle it. When he steps into the God-Author it is to relay "non-fiction" information to the reader. It takes the story from showing to telling, which he has done on purpose for the effect and he always rounds the "non-fiction information" back into the story.

For now, take away the point that the God-Author always tells a story rather than showing.

The opposite end of the spectrum is first person. We live every day in first person: <u>I</u> went to the store in <u>my</u> car and <u>my</u> brother went with <u>me</u>. But how often do we really pay attention to our own thoughts and hear our own inner conversations?

It's this very fact that makes writing in first person seem deceptively easy, but remarkably hard. The biggest challenge is that you can't hide thoughts from yourself. You may consciously choose not to think about something and this may work for a while, but if you know something, you <u>know something</u>.

I very nearly put *Twilight* down in the first few pages because first person Bella kept hinting at there being a reason behind her decision to go live with her dad, but it takes her several times before she says what that reason is. By page seven I wanted a new hook; this one was getting old. Bella <u>knew</u> her reason so she was hiding from the reader, not herself. It destroyed the first person perception. You can't keep skirting around the issue while never quite realizing the whole thought so many times.

Another severe drawback of first person is the fact that you cannot tell the story from any external character. Oh, I've seen it tried, where the author has another 'I' character or even switches to third person to show what's happening elsewhere. Both are sloppy and signs of a story that isn't well thought out and structured. If you are going to use first person, stick with that character for the duration of the story. If you're going to use third person, it's best to stay with one character per scene. If you have to use more than one in a scene, make sure your transitions are smooth by remembering to think in a cinematic fashion.

A final thing on point of view: if your character has a nickname, know how each of the characters around your main character refers to the nicknamed character. If your character is Jimmy John, but everyone refers to him as JJ, don't have his mother call him Jimmy, JJ, and Jimmy John in the same conversation. Mother is going to have a favorite name. Maybe she doesn't even like the nickname; she may despise it. On the other hand, she may call him JJ under normal circumstances and call him Jimmy John if she's being sharp with him. It's the difference between, "You're a good boy, JJ, for opening the door for the lady" and "Jimmy John, be a good boy and open the door for the lady."

Now that you know what makes good point of view, you'll be finding errors in every book you read. You may even think, "They get away with it. Why can't I?" You are the better author, remember? Strive for consistency in your point of view and you'll be at the head of the pack for the new generation of writers.

Narrative:

What Happens in the Silence?

Narrative, as you know, is all the stuff that goes on when your characters aren't speaking. Let's discuss the problem areas.

Controlling pace is an important aspect of narrative. Here's an example:

Sheriff Rogers spotted the robbers heading into the bank. He dismounted and draped his reins over the hitching post, briefly knotting them. He sped across the street and threw open the bank's door. Already the robbers had everyone in the building on the floor. Rogers looked around. The teller had his hands in the air. Papers were scattered around the room among overturned chairs and desks. Dappled sunlight spilled through the barred windows, casting long shadows on the floor and striping the wooden floor. Mr. Jenkins, a stout balding man wearing a pin stripped suit, cowered behind his overturned desk while sweat beaded his forehead. Gun shots rang out, bringing Rogers back to the moment at hand. He had to do something and quick. He dove behind a wooden chair and used it as a shield. Raising his gun, Rogers fired back.

Not a bad start for a first draft, but definitely needs work.

For starters, the words are too soft. Do you think someone who's just seen robbers go into a bank is going to 'drape' his reins over the hitching post? What about the adverb 'briefly'? Again, it's too soft of a word.

Let's try that again:

The moment Sheriff Rogers saw the robbers entering the bank, he knotted his horse to the hitching post and sped across the road.

Still not perfect, but better. Let's keep going and see what develops.

The next problem is that Rogers opens the door, sees everyone on the ground, and then looks around. There's a bit of a sequencing problem there. He should open the door, look around, and see all the people on the ground. Also, when he does look around, the description of what he sees brings the story to a dead stop. Nothing moves in this span where he looks around. Do you think that bad guys are going to stand by and let the good sheriff assess the situation?

Here's where you face a dilemma. We know we don't want to stop the story dead in its tracks. But, considering this is part of an action sequence, do we want to slow down the pace some or do we keep high action going from the moment Rogers ties up his horse?

For the sake of illustration, let's keep up the high action:

The moment Sheriff Rogers saw the robbers entering the bank, he knotted his horse to the hitching post and sped across the road. He kicked in the door and drew his gun. Dropping to the floor, he rolled into the bank. Shots fired. Scared bank patrons screamed. Rogers scrambled behind and overturned chair. He raised his gun and fired back.

During high action scenes short sentences move your story along quickly, but our paragraph moves too fast. Aside from the acrobatics of the main character, do you really see anything else? I call this 'white room syndrome' and it's what happens when there are not enough setting details. In this paragraph, we don't see any of the bank's interior except the overturned chair which pops into existence when needed.

So, high action isn't appropriate here. There are times to use it, but only after setting is firmly established or if a character is in a confused state. Let's try this scene again:

The moment Sheriff Rogers saw the robbers entering the bank, he knotted his horse to the hitching post and sped across the dirt road.

Sunlight entering through the barred windows allowed Rogers to see the bank patrons on the wooden floor among the stripped shadows. Arms and legs intermixed with overturned chairs and desks. Sweat beaded on Mr. Jenkins' bald forehead. Jenkins' fingers shook as he pulled a handkerchief from the pocket of his pinstriped suit.

Rogers raised his gun and dove inside the bank, rolling behind a fallen chair. Gunshots blasted. Rogers returned fire.

Better, but notice how the second paragraph still stops the story. Also notice that Rogers never opens the bank door. Did you notice, or did you assume? Did the robbers even close the door after they entered or did they leave it open for a quick get away? I intentionally let the assumption hang as it's probably not a necessary action requiring narrative. Merely having Rogers cross the street, then having a paragraph break before mentioning what's going on inside the bank is enough of a transition to clue the reader unconsciously.

In this day and age of blogging where 'white space' is what you put between sentences to give the reader breathing room and reduce eye strain, it's important that writers realize what important tools they have been given with something as simple as a paragraph break. This is why you must get your story out so you can come back into the second or third draft to see the structure of the words without worrying about the story. You can't divide your brain during that initial writing phase to do both story and structure. Trying to do so is what causes all those right brain, left brain fights. Let each side have their turn in the proper order.

Let's try this example one last time:

The moment Sheriff Rogers saw the robbers entering the bank, he knotted his horse to the hitching post and sped across the dirt road. He stood at the edge of the open door and peeked inside.

Mr. Jenkins, the bank president, cowered among his papers behind his overturned desk in the striped shadows of sunlight coming through the barred windows.

He saw Rogers and motioned him to come inside the bank.

Rogers pressed a finger to his lips, afraid that Jenkins would call out to him. He needed a little more time to assess the situation. Jenkins seemed to understand and pulled a handkerchief from the pocket of his pinstriped suit to wipe sweat from his balding head.

On the floor, a woman whimpered as she covered her head with her arms. For a moment, Rogers thought it might draw the attention of the robbers, but they remained focused on the teller shoving cash into their bags.

Rogers drew his gun. He slipped inside, staying near the wall. If he could...

A wooden floorboard beneath his boot creaked and the robbers turned in alarm. Rogers returned fire as he dove behind an overturned chair. Patrons screamed as shots ricocheted.

A bullet struck the chair near Rogers' head and the wood splintered. Rogers took aim from behind his makeshift shield and squeezed the trigger. The shot landed and the robber fell.

Notice how in this draft it's mentioned that Rogers stands at the open door, indicating that the robbers hadn't closed it on their way in. Is it necessary? Probably not, except that it clues the reader in that it's slightly ajar when Jenkins sees him. It's a good detail. The desks, papers, wooden floor, pinstriped suit, patrons, striped shadows, and patrons are all still in here, but notice how each bit of description is doing something. Mr. Jenkins is with his papers cowering behind his desk. This speaks volumes about the man and how his papers, his business, are important to him. The wooden floor serves as an alarm. Patrons are whimpering, and then screaming. I still don't feel like this scene is as

43

rich as it could be, but it points you in the right direction.

Don't just sprinkle in description; make it part of the scene. If you want to tell me that Carolyn has brown hair, don't write, 'Carolyn had curly brown hair and stood five foot eight inches.' Instead write, 'Carolyn ducked through the doorway and her curly hair fell forward into her face. She tucked back an unruly, brown strand behind her ear as she said, "Why did they make doorways so small a hundred years ago?"'

This brings us to the most important point of this book: show, don't tell.

How do you know the difference between telling and showing? The words 'was,' 'could,' 'would' and the lot of similar "to be" verbs are your first clue. While it's impossible to completely do away with them (you'll notice one 'would' in the last bank example), it's when they appear in clusters that you should recognize the problem immediately. Let's take the following example:

Kultha was running down the street. Her heart was pounding, her feet slapping against the cobblestone road. Her red robes were snapping around her ankles.

I've underlined the words so that you can see the cluster. Go through your own text and look for these clusters. The goal is to get rid of all of them that you can. Let's see how this can be done.

Kultha raced down the street glancing back over her shoulder. Her heart pounded and her red robes snapped around her ankles as her feet slapped against the cobblestone road.

Sometimes it's just a matter of changing the verb to an -ed ending or making it past tense.

'Was running' becomes 'ran,' 'was pounding' becomes 'pounded.' Other times it's a matter of rearranging your words. Let's look at an example like that:

The doorway of the ruined cottage was hidden behind a tangle of brush while the window was scratched with a pine branch.

Edited:

A tangle of brush hid the doorway of the ruined cottage while a pine branch scratched against the window.

Reversing the order quickly takes care of the inactive verbs, making them active.

Backstory is one area where there's no way around inactive verbs. While they can't be eliminated, they can be reduced. Let's look at a potential opening scene:

The truck was sitting in the middle of the road. Frank knew he should have turned back before his tires were stuck in the mud, but here he sat. He could've apologized to Anne before it got this bad and he wouldn't now be stranded halfway to nowhere. The night was growing cold as well as dark. His jacket wasn't going to be enough to keep him warm through the night.

Again I've underlined the inactive verbs in this. Now let's reduce all of them that we can, while still leaving in the backstory elements that the reader needs to know.

Frank pulled his jacket closer around him, wondering if it'd keep him warm enough through the night as he sat in the truck half way up its wheels in the mud. It's not like he could go back and apologize to Anne now, not stranded halfway to nowhere.

The two important backstory elements are that Frank is stuck in his truck and he had a fight with Anne. Even though we don't know who Anne is, the reader can bet that Anne and the subject of their fight will soon be revealed. Because, if these items aren't coming, why are you showing them?

Make sure if it makes it in your text, that it's relevant. There's a rule you can count on. It's called the rule of three. Basically, if you show something, you must use it. If you draw attention to a gun in someone's dresser drawer, then you should use it in the end. Otherwise it's irrelevant, so why bring it up? To appropriately show the rule of three, you should show the gun in the drawer, then show it in the hands of one of your character, then that character needs to fire it before the end of the book. Not everything has to follow the rule of three, but it should if it's important. That's what builds tension. The reader, sometimes subconsciously, knows it's coming. The question is: when will it happen?

I'm certain you've heard of a story twist. This is how you make it happen. The reader knows it's coming, but not when. If you make what the reader is expecting happen in an unexpected way, you have a twist. And yes, you can plan these out.

Planning out a twist is nothing more than knowing what your reader expects. Write it happening that way, maybe expanding beyond that planned event, then go back and figure out how to alter it with a surprise. Sometimes this means rewriting earlier scenes so that your changes fall in naturally. If you can get these plotted out in-between writing your first and second synopsis, you'll save yourself a heap load of time. Sometimes it doesn't happen this way. If you do end up rewriting, don't whine about having to go back and put it in. Just go do it. There's no sense in complaining about making your story better when you can get it done.

By now, you should sense that if you've been looking for someone to coddle your writing along, you've come to the wrong place. Too much time has been wasted by every writer, including myself, on whining about this or that. Time that is better spent writing.

Dialogue:

You said what?

I mentioned earlier that we rarely listen to the actual thoughts we think. In some ways, the same could be said for dialogue. But because we all speak, dialogue comes naturally for most authors if it's just characters acting/reacting to each other.

Dialogue can have another purpose though. It can be used effectively to pass along backstory. Let's take this example:

Dad looked out the window above the kitchen sink. "Who's that driving in?"

Jenni followed his gaze to see the red truck kicking up dust in their driveway and turned to grab her red backpack for school and black dance bag. "It's Casey's."

"Casey's? I didn't know Mr. Vedder could afford a payment for a new truck? He should've stopped by to see me."

"I don't think Mr. Vedder brought it. I think it was a present from her biological father, Rick Palmer."

What have we learned from the dialogue here? We learned that Jenni's father knows Casey well enough to only call Casey by her first name, otherwise he would've said "Casey Vedder?" We know that Casey's mom is divorced or had a daughter out of wedlock and that Casey's father is Rick Palmer. We know that the Vedders probably don't have a whole lot of money. And we know that Jenni's dad is either a car salesman or is in car financing. That's a lot of information passed to the reader in four short paragraphs. The reader won't always pick up all this information in just one reading. If it's important that the Vedders don't have much money, you'll need to find other ways to reiterate this to the reader. But only focus on what's important; so again, reinforce it if it's important to your story, delete it if it's not relevant.

Be careful when you're revealing dialogue that your characters don't become talking heads. This occurs when there is only dialogue with little or no narrative to break it up. Dialogue and narrative need to be a skillful dance, playing off one another. If you find yourself dialogue heavy, which means characters talking for more than five paragraphs, look at what is being revealed and ask yourself if there's another way or place to get the information out.

How about thoughts as dialogue? My first preference is don't do it. We've learned how easy it is to change first person thoughts to third person narrative. But if you're using first person, then you'll have to use interior thoughts. Just remember that thoughts are a solo form of dialogue. Often a person will ask an internal question and answer it too with hardly a breath between them.

If I can't convince you to not use thoughts in a third person story, please, I beg you, don't use thoughts from secondary characters. If you absolutely must use thoughts, reserve it for your main character. Be skillful enough to show your secondary characters' thoughts through their actions and dialogue. If you include thoughts from other characters, you'll be head jumping again with your point of view and we all know what a bumpy ride that is.

Off to a great start!

Your first page is the most critical.

When I'm judging a contest, I can tell within the first two paragraphs if I'm going to like a story or not, if a writer knows how to write or not. If I know this, so do editors. We've all heard the stories of editors and/or assistant editors sitting around Friday night with pizza and going through the slush pile. We all know how important it is to get out of the slush pile and into an editor's hands. Make them put that pizza down to turn the page of your manuscript.

Which is stronger: 'He stepped out into the street, a confident air about his stride' or 'Steven stepped out into the street, a confident air about his stride'? I'm betting you said the second one.

Don't start off with a pronoun. Only one word changed between the two sentences. Story is about character and you want to identify your character as soon as you can. If you start by disconnecting your reader from the character, the reader will never truly care. Remove all barriers that might keep your reader from identifying with your character. Otherwise you threaten the emotional bond and if you want the reader to sympathize with your character, you need to grow this connection quickly.

Never use 'was' in the first paragraph, preferably the first two paragraphs. Remember that 'was' is the first clue that a story is being told, not shown Now, your assignment is to pick up some of the newest "literature" being released and see if they break this rule, then look a little deeper to see if the story is being told or shown. Yes, it's happening in books being published today. Unfortunately, most of these books probably had an agent behind them and didn't come from the slush pile. Whether or not you have an agent, you should always strive to give the reader the best book you can. If you expect them to lay out good money for your book, then make sure you give them a good read showing a story, not telling one. This means avoiding 'was' as much as you can.

The last thing you can do to keep your readers reading is to show your character doing something strong. If you show a character sitting at a table crying without the reader having an emotional connection, the reader will not care about the character's tears. In fact, the character will seem whiny and weak no matter what the character was crying about. Let's say the character had been crying over the loss of her father, that he died recently and your main character is missing him. While we all can sympathize with this situation, being an outside observer without any knowledge of the character or her father, it's easy for the reader to stay detached. More importantly, it probably means that your story has started in the wrong place.

Wouldn't it be a much better story to show the character and her father interacting in a scene illustrating the strength of their love before having the character crying at the table?

If your hero is a skilled swordsman, don't show him losing a fight. In fact, don't show him losing any competition. Show him winning, even if it's a minor event.

People like winners. The reader knows the character is going to face a danger and wants to know the character has a chance to win. If the lead is weak, the reader won't believe it's possible for the character to overcome against the danger.

It's a tall order to get done in the first few paragraphs, but if you take care with the words of your story, your work will be noticed.

The next section is a sample for you to edit. You may want to photocopy it so you can use it a couple of times for practice. The last page is how I edited the page. Your page doesn't have to be the same as mine, nor is it expected to be the same as long as you are catching the main elements.

Good writing is always good writing. That fact will never change.

I hope your writing is the best ever!

Sample Practice

"Don't take this personally, but I hate you." She was glaring at the knight standing in the hallway with his red and gold armor sparkling in the light. "I have work to do."

Katlyn, carrying a bundle of bed sheets, stepped around Daelik, intentionally bumping her shoulder against him even though she knew his armor would leave a bruise. She dropped the sheets in the hallway at the feet of a second man, Brom, standing there dressed in long black robes.

"Always a pleasure, milady." Daelik strolled into the bedchamber knowing he had every right to be there. <u>She's certainly being a wench today,</u> he thought.

"Are there books in here?" Brom whispered out of the side of his mouth.

Katlyn was looking him straight in the

eye, her lips were tight, and she gave him a minimal nod. Then turning, she noticed Daelik was doing in her bedchamber. "Excuse me." She rushed into her room, took a dagger from his hand, and set it carefully back down on a flat stone covered with crystals, candles, and little statues. "You have no right to touch anything on my altar."

Daelik cocked his head to the side and smiled. He was a couple years older than Katlyn, had rugged features, with piercing green eyes and bright golden hair. "Your father told me to come in here and have a look," he said.

"Is that so?" Katlyn put a hand on her hip and gave him a stare that made most people wither. Unfortunately, it came back to him being too stupid to realize when he was getting The Look.

"Yes, to make sure your dagger was still on the altar, and not under your gown."

Dawn Blair

Sample Practice - My Edit

"Don't take this personally, but I hate you." ~~She was glaring~~ *Katlyn glared* at the knight standing in the ~~hallway~~ *castle* with his red and gold armor sparkling in the ~~light~~ *torch* light. "I have work to do."

The knight's green eyes shone with ⟨mischief⟩ - HC needs a harder word

~~Katlyn~~ *She*, carrying a bundle of ~~bed sheets~~ *clothes*, stepped around Daelik, intentionally bumping her shoulder against him even though she knew his armor would leave a bruise *on her arms*.

She dropped the ~~sheets~~ *clothes* in the ~~hallway at the feet~~ of a second man, Brom, standing there dressed in long black robes.

— need to mention Brom earlier - he pops into existence - him + brief description

"Always a pleasure, milady." Daelik strolled into the bedchamber ~~knowing he~~ *like he* had every right to be there. ~~She's certainly being a wench today,~~ *he thought.*

"Are there books in here?" Brom whispered ~~out of the side of his mouth.~~

Katlyn ~~was looking~~ *looked* him straight in the eye, her lips ~~were~~ tight, and she gave him a minimal nod. Then turning, she noticed Daelik ~~was doing in her bedchamber.~~ *by her altar. (extra space)* "Excuse me." She rushed into her room, ~~took a~~ *⟨stormed⟩? snatched the* dagger from his hand, and ~~set it carefully~~ *(back)* *unspecific.* down on a flat stone covered with crystals, candles, and little statues. "You have no right to touch anything ~~on my altar.~~"

— show this - flat- I see her doing this with thumb + forefinger on the hilt + the flat of the blade.

A strand of golden blond hair fell against Daelik's cheek as he
~~Daelik~~ cocked his head to the side and smiled. ~~He was a couple years older than~~

~~Katlyn, had rugged features, with piercing green eyes and bright golden hair.~~ "Your father told me to come in here and have a look," he said.

"Is that so?" ~~Katlyn put a~~ *Katlyn glowered at* hand on her hip, ~~and gave him a stare that made most~~ *wishing to make him withes.*

~~people with a. Unfortunately, it came back to him being too stupid to realize when he~~

~~was getting The Look.~~
Daelik smiled, but instead of softening his sharp features, it gave them more of an edge.
"Yes, to make sure your dagger was still on the altar, and not under your gown."

Setting- She's in the doorway with the sheets in her arms.

This may need to come before first line.

62

Special Treat

Now that you've seen my edit, come and listen to why I made the choices that I did. There's a special, free companion podcast to accompany this book just for you. Go to **www.morningskystudios.com/podcast** then click the link for The Write Edit Companion Podcast. Listen online or download to your computer or MP3 player. It's about 10 minutes long and gives additional hands-on insight into how I work through an edit. Enjoy.

9 7 8 0 9 8 3 0 9 0 5 6 4